"This is a book that churches should be handing out in bulk for Advent. With lucid biblical content, helpful application and superb prayers for each day, it surges with the comfort and joy of Christmas."

**Michael Reeves,**
*Director of Union and Senior Lecturer at*
*Wales Evangelical School of Theology*

"It's a sad paradox in the Christian life that, at the very time when we should be full of joyful anticipation of Christ's coming, we are often at our most jaded, tired and cynical. In a compelling, fresh and concise way, Tim Chester provides a wonderful selection of readings which will inspire our weary hearts and refresh our vision of Jesus. Following these daily readings will be a great preparation for a Christ-focussed Christmas."

**Jonathan Lamb,**
*CEO and Minister-at-Large, Keswick Ministries*

"If you're looking for a fresh, creative, insightful, and thoroughly biblical and Christ-exalting guide for Advent, look no further. Tim Chester's book, *The One True Light*, applies biblical theology to the first 18 verses of John's Gospel to show us how the incarnation affects every aspect of our lives. Brief and simple enough for children, yet deep and rich enough for mature Christians, this is a book that inspires awe, wonder, and praise for Emmanuel, God with us."

**Bob Kauflin,**
*Director of Sovereign Grace Music*

"In this short, accessible book, we are invited to 'join John in fixing our eyes on Jesus, the one true light'. As I read it, that's exactly what I found myself doing. Buy it and read it. Buy another and give it as a gift. It's an investment not an expense."

**Steve Timmis,**
*Executive Director, Acts 29*

Tim Chester

# The One True Light

Daily readings for Advent
from the Gospel of John

The One True Light
© Tim Chester/The Good Book Company, 2015

Published by
The Good Book Company
Tel (UK): 0333 123 0880
International: +44 (0) 208 942 0880
Email: info@thegoodbook.co.uk

Websites:
UK: www.thegoodbook.co.uk
North America: www.thegoodbook.com
Australia: www.thegoodbook.com.au
New Zealand: www.thegoodbook.co.nz

ISBN: 9781910307991

Design by André Parker

Printed in the UK

# Contents

# Approaching Christmas

I used to be a big curmudgeon about Christmas. Not quite Ebenezer Scrooge—but close.

I moaned about the rubbish on the television. I moaned about the terrible Christmas songs that get repeated every year. I moaned about all the tatty decorations—tinsel and snow globes and illuminated reindeers. In my mind, Christmas was unavoidably associated with the oppressive warmth of my in-laws' home.

In my high-minded moments I moaned about the commercialism that seems to be replacing the Christmas message. Or I moaned about versions of Christmas that sanitise Jesus and make him "safe".

But, of course, by "high-minded" I really mean "self-righteous". I used to be a curmudgeon—a proud one.

However, I've noticed a change over the past few years. As I slide into middle age, I've somewhat given up the fight. I let Christmas happen to me. I embrace the festivities. I even sometimes allow myself to have fun.

But, whether being curmudgeonly or celebratory, it is easy to get distracted from the wonder of God becoming man. The build-up to Christmas is a busy time. There are presents to buy, parties to attend, food to prepare, cards to send and relatives to visit.

So it's easy to forget about Jesus, even at Christmas—*especially* at Christmas. But the truth is that we'll never enjoy Christmas properly unless we understand who it is who was born in Bethlehem that night. Indeed, we won't enjoy life to the full until we see God in a manger.

In these Advent readings, we're going to look at John's version of the Christmas story. It's not the Christmas story as we've come to expect it. There's no stable, no donkey and no star. There are no angels, no shepherds and no wise men. Even Mary and Joseph don't get a look in. Instead the focus is entirely on Jesus, the God-become-man. This is Christmas stripped bare. All that's left is Jesus. And that's all you need to make your December explode with joy, and your life revolve around the One who brings truth, life, community, reality, clarity—light.

So by all means make sure you've bought your presents, ordered the turkey, attended your parties and ticked off seeing the relatives. But see the 24 daily readings in this book as an opportunity to focus not on the to-do list, or even on Christmas as such, but on Christ—to join John in fixing your eyes on Jesus, the one true light.

∽

# In the beginning

*"In the beginning..."*
John 1 v 1

My father's father was a butcher from North Yorkshire. He would collect animals from the train and then drive them through the village to be slaughtered behind his shop. My mother's father was Scottish. He moved to Darlington in County Durham to work at the steel mill. He would come home each evening with livid burns up his arms...

Many biographies start a generation or two back with the subject's parents or grandparents. The aim is to build a picture of the kind of family and conditions a child was born into.

Not John's Gospel.

As John settles down to write the story of a man called Jesus, he thinks of his earthly parents, and of their fathers and forefathers. But the clock keeps spinning backwards until he draws breath and slowly writes, *"In the beginning"*.

Immediately, we understand that this is not an ordinary story of an ordinary person.

John's "in the beginning" is not the start of one person's life. This is the start and source of all life. This is the story of creation. The words echo the opening words of the opening book of the Bible. Genesis 1 v 1 reads, "In the beginning God created the heavens and the earth". John is retelling the story of creation with Jesus the Word at the centre.

So this is a big story. It's not the story of *one* person, but of *every* person. This is *my* story. And *your* story. This is the story of the universe, and specifically of planet earth.

∾

The story of creation in Genesis 1 came to a climax when God formed the first human being, Adam. John's "Christmas story" will also come to a climax with a man taking on human flesh. Genesis shows us the first man—Adam. But Jesus will be "the last Adam". In both cases a man enters the world. Jesus is coming as the true Adam or the true man.

But Jesus is more than a new, improved human being. This is not simply *"Humanity 2.0"*. John could have started with the story of the birth of Jesus. That's what Matthew and Luke do. But John wants us to realise that, unlike the story of any other human being, the story of Jesus does not begin with his human conception. It's true that Jesus was born as a human being in our world. But that's not when his story begins. His story goes back to the beginning. Indeed the story of Jesus doesn't even start "in the beginning". For, as John will go on to say, Jesus already "was" in the beginning. His story has no beginning for he "was" in eternity. He has been for ever.

∾

Did you know that Santa once threw a punch? The name "Santa Claus" is derived from "Saint Nicholas". Nicholas was a bishop who attended the Council of Nicea in AD 325. The council had been called in response to the teaching of a man called Arius, who claimed that Jesus was a created being. He was willing to affirm that Jesus was the first created being and so supreme in creation, but, according to Arius, he was created. In other words, there was a time when Jesus did not exist.

The story goes that at first Nicholas listened quietly to the arguments of Arius. But in the end he could take it no longer. He stepped across the room and slapped Arius across the face. So maybe on Christmas Day we should punch heretics instead of giving presents. (Or maybe not.)

The point is that this truth mattered deeply to Nicholas. It was not just a debating point—it was of crucial importance for the salvation of our souls. If Jesus was created, then he is not truly and fully divine. And John is clear: Jesus the Word already "was" in the beginning.

But why does John start here, looking back to the beginning of creation? Because the story John is about to unfold is the story of *re-creation*. The world God made is no longer the same world in which we live. God made a good world, a beautiful world. And there are still signs of that all around us. But there is also evil and pain.

Our world is broken. And we are the ones who broke it.

John starts "in the beginning" to give us a hint of what Jesus will do. Jesus is going to mend the brokenness of our world. The story of creation went into reverse when humanity rejected God. Creation gave way to de-creation. God's beautiful world began to unravel. But Jesus is about to pick up the pen, as it were, and write the next chapter—another chapter of creation.

## Meditate
*In the beginning…*

*Of the Father's love begotten,*
*Ere the worlds began to be,*
*He is Alpha and Omega,*
*He the source, the ending he,*
*Of the things that are, that have been,*
*And that future years shall see,*
*Evermore and evermore!*
*(Of the Father's Love Begotten)*

∽

## Prayer
*Lord Jesus,*
*thank you that you have rewritten the story,*
*thank you that you are reordering our world.*
*In your mercy,*
*come and rewrite my story;*
*come and reorder my world.*
*Amen.*

# The 2 Word

*"In the beginning was the Word…"*
John 1 v 1

Have you ever wrapped a Christmas present for your cat? Have you ever watched a TV programme simply because you didn't want to disturb the cat on your lap by reaching for the remote? Have you ever stood shivering at an open door while your cat decided whether it wanted to go out? Are you a cat person?

I live among cat people. We live under the delusion that we own our cat. But our cat acts as if she owns us. And our next door neighbour. And pretty much everything and anyone she comes into contact with…

Personally, I'm more of a dog person. Dogs appear to understand a wider vocabulary of human words and pick up on our emotions more. Maybe cats understand as much, but they just don't care. We can have some kind of meaningful relationship with a dog. But even with dogs, we can't do things like share our hopes for the future.

So what about single-celled organisms like bacteria? You already have millions of them as pets: in your house, on your body and in your gut. But imagine trying to communicate with your pet bacteria. Imagine them sitting on the back of your hand now. How do you speak to them? You can't write a letter. They can't follow you on Twitter. You could whisper to them, or even shout. But can they hear? And how would you know that the message had got through? I guess you could do the chemical equivalent of poking them. But it's hardly meaningful communication. They don't know your name or the names of your family.

And even if you could get through to them, what language would you speak? Even if you could say something, would they understand any of the concepts you used?

Suppose you manage to say, "I'm just off for brunch with my family". Would they understand what brunch is? Or a family? Or even what it means to be a conscious individual, an "I"? Probably not. (Or maybe they would ask you to pass on regards to their extended family living in your partly-cooked burgers!)

We can have a limited relationship with a dog. But any meaningful relationship with a bacterium is impossible because *we are just too different.*

∽

This is something like the problem involved in God communicating with humanity, because God and humanity are so different. Before God we're the equivalent of bacteria on a Petri dish. How can God communicate to us? What language can he use? Even if we could hear words from him, how could he say anything that we could comprehend?

The goods news is that Jesus is *the Word of God,* in whom we hear

God. John's Gospel begins, "In the beginning was the Word". The man Jesus, says John, is the Word. God has accommodated himself to us in the most incredible way. He has become one of us. It's as if I transformed myself into a bacterium to communicate with other bacteria.

Think for a moment about doing that. Think about the massive implications that would have for you. Think of everything you would give up. Think of the incomprehension of others at your choice. Think of how strong the driving force would need to be for you to make that choice.

∼

What does that choice mean for us? We can't see Jesus in the flesh. We can't hear him teaching by Lake Galilee or see him performing a miracle. Do you ever wish you had been there, standing in the boat as water ran across your feet, feeling your stomach turn with the swell of the waves, smelling the spray as sweat ran down your face? And then hearing the words, "Be still"?

But we weren't there and we can't hear the calm, commanding voice of Jesus. We can't stand open-mouthed in fearful wonder as the waves lie flat at the sound of his voice. So how can we hear God today?

The answer is that we can encounter Jesus the Word in the promises of the prophets in the Old Testament and the testimony of the apostles in the New Testament. The Spirit-inspired Bible gives us access to Jesus the Word. We encounter him as his story is retold. We encounter him as his message is preached. We encounter the Word in the words of Scripture.

And whenever we encounter him, we encounter God. Whenever we hear the message of Jesus, we hear the voice of God.

*Tim Chester*

## Meditate
*In the beginning was the Word...*

*Yea, Lord, we greet thee, born that happy morning;*
*Jesus, to thee be glory given!*
*Word of the Father, now in flesh appearing!*
*O come, let us adore him,*
*O come, let us adore him,*
*O come, let us adore him,*
*Christ the Lord.*
*(O Come, All Ye Faithful)*

~

## Prayer
*Blessed Lord,*
*who has caused all holy Scriptures to be written for our learning:*
*Grant that we may in such wise hear them,*
*read, mark, learn, and inwardly digest them,*
*that by patience and comfort of your holy Word,*
*we may embrace, and ever hold fast*
*the blessed hope of everlasting life,*
*which you have given us in our Saviour Jesus Christ.*
*Amen.*
*(The Book of Common Prayer,*
*the Collect for the second Sunday in Advent)*

# With God–was God
### 3

*"And the Word was with God,*
*and the Word was God.*
*He was with God in the beginning."*
John 1 v 1–2

S o which is it, John? Was the Word *with* God, or was the Word *God*? Because surely it can't be both.

I can't say, "Helen is with my wife and Helen is my wife." The phrase "Helen is with my wife" describes two people. But "Helen is my wife" describes just one person. The only way to make this statement work is if there are two people who are *both* called Helen.

But John isn't talking about two Words. *"The Word"* is different from God (and therefore able to be with him) and the Word is the *same as* God. Surely the Word is either with God or is God.

Unless… unless we are talking about a being who is completely different from us.

∾

In Greek thought, the "word" or "reason" was the organising principle behind the world. It may be that John has an echo of this in mind as he writes. But it's more likely that to the fore is the Old Testament use of the term "word". John himself was Jewish and his Gospel is full of allusions to the Old Testament. John repeatedly draws attention to the way Jesus fulfils the promises and patterns of the Scriptures.

And in the Old Testament God's word is the means by which God speaks and acts. Indeed God's word is synonymous with God.

We have a sense of this as human beings. We have an organic connection with our words. Suppose you complained to me, "But you said you would help". I couldn't reply, "No I didn't—that was just my words". Our words are more than sounds, or pixels in an email. They represent our thoughts and intentions. They convey our very selves.

Except, of course, that our words don't always convey ourselves truly. The 2002 movie *Catch Me If You Can* tells the true story of Frank Abagnale, played by Leonardo DiCaprio. Abagnale was a con-man who at different points successfully passed himself off as a pilot, a doctor and a legal prosecutor. He certainly had a way with words. His words were very powerful. But his words didn't convey his true self—they were lies.

But God is perfect and so his word is perfect. And that means his word is a perfect representation of his being. God's word is such a complete revelation of himself that *it is himself.* God's word conveys who he is and it does so perfectly.

∽

The Word is with God because the Word is Jesus, the Son of God. And God is three Persons. Jesus is not the Father. They're different persons. So Jesus the Word *can be* with God. God the Son is *with* God the Father without *being* God the Father. John doesn't say Jesus is God as if there are no other Persons in the Godhead.

At the same time the Word *is* God because there aren't three gods. The Father is God and Jesus is God. Father, Son and Spirit are one divine Being.

*Why does this matter?* It means that God can communicate in a way that is sure and true. When we hear God's Word, we don't just hear a second-hand report about God. We hear God himself because his Word is God.

Of course there is still much we don't know. The Trinity is so much bigger than anything we can get our heads round.

You know the story of the baby born in the stable who was visited by three kings? Wrong. There's no mention of a stable. We're only told Jesus was laid in a *manger*. And there weren't three kings. There were an unnamed number of "Magi"—whatever they are. Yet however well you know the details of the Christmas story, you only know the half of it; for the Christmas story begins in the life of the Trinity, and that is a mystery beyond our comprehension.

We cannot know God fully. But we can know him truly, for Jesus is the Word, through whom we hear the voice of God.

### Meditate

*And the Word was with God,*
*and the Word was God.*
*He was with God in the beginning.*

*Christ, by highest heav'n adored;*
*Christ the everlasting Lord;*
*Late in time, behold him come,*
*Offspring of a virgin's womb.*
*Veiled in flesh the Godhead see;*

*Hail th'incarnate Deity,*
*Pleased as man with man to dwell,*
*Jesus, our Emmanuel.*
*(Hark the Herald Angels Sing)*

~

## Prayer
*Good morning heavenly Father,*
*good morning Lord Jesus,*
*good morning Holy Spirit.*

*Heavenly Father, I worship you as the Creator and Sustainer of the universe.*
*Lord Jesus, I worship you, Saviour and Lord of the world.*
*Holy Spirit, I worship you, Sanctifier of the people of God.*
*Glory to the Father, and to the Son and to the Holy Spirit.*

*Heavenly Father, I pray that I may live this day*
*in your presence and please you more and more.*
*Lord Jesus, I pray that this day I may take up my cross and follow you.*
*Holy Spirit, I pray that this day you will fill me with yourself*
*and cause your fruit to ripen in my life:*
*love, joy, peace, patience, kindness,*
*goodness, faithfulness, gentleness and self-control.*
*Holy, blessed and glorious Trinity, three persons in one God,*
*have mercy upon me. Amen.*
*(The Morning Prayer of John Stott, 1921-2011)*

# Let there be 4

*"Through him all things were made;*
*without him nothing was made*
*that has been made."*
John 1 v 3

Sometimes my words are quite powerful. I've quietened a room of people through my words. I've made people laugh through my words. And cry.

I've made a marriage through my words. I've even silenced Emily Jenkins with my words. And if you knew three-year-old Emily, then you would understand what an achievement that is.

The Word that John is introducing to us is powerful. Jesus is the Word, through whom we hear God's voice. But this Word is not just about *communication*; he is also about *creation*. Jesus is also the Word through whom God made the world.

John begins with a deliberate echo of the opening of Genesis: "In the beginning", as we saw when we looked at verse 1. John is retelling the story of creation with Jesus the Word at the centre.

In Genesis 1, God spoke and the world came into being. "And God said, 'Let there be light,' and there was light"

(Genesis 1 v 3). The psalmist says that, "By the word of the LORD were the heavens made, their starry host by the breath of his mouth" (Psalm 33 v 6). My words can be powerful. But I've never made a tree with my words. Or the heavens. Or their starry host.

God spoke and the universe came into existence. And the word that God spoke was Jesus. Through him all things were made; without him nothing was made that has been made.

We can't understand the mechanics of this act. But God the Father spoke, the Word he spoke was Jesus and through that Word the world was created. Creation took place through the mediation of the Son. The Father is the architect and Jesus is the plan. Jesus is the model, the prototype, the pattern of creation.

∾

There's a lovely description of the process of creation in Proverbs 8. Wisdom personified speaks. It is, I think, a picture of Jesus. Jesus describes how he witnessed creation and then adds: "Then I was beside him, like a master workman, and I was daily his delight, rejoicing before him always, rejoicing in his inhabited world and delighting in the children of man" (Proverbs 8 v 30-31, English Standard Version translation).

The image is of Father and Son working side by side. The Father conceives and plans the world in all its beauty and complexity. And Jesus is the master workman constructing the plan of the Father.

And did you notice that they're having fun together? The Son *delights* in the plan of the Father. The Father *delights* in the execution of that plan by the Son. Why? Because the Son *himself* is the plan. "*I* was daily his delight." We might almost imagine the Son saying to the Father, "I love what you've planned for these mountains. Wow, that waterfall is amazing." And the Father says to the Son,

"You've done an amazing job with those dragonflies—that's lovely workmanship."

Jesus rejoices in the world they are making together. And he especially delights in humanity because we are made in the image of the triune God. More than anywhere else, this is where Jesus sees his Father's glory reflected in creation.

∽

Jesus is that Word through whom God creates. And this is what we're going to see played out in the rest of John's Gospel. John is trailing his story.

We're not going to see acts of creation—that work has been done. But we are going to see acts of *re-creation*. We're going to see Jesus commanding the waves, feeding the hungry and restoring the sick.

Jesus is not just a preacher or a healer. He is the Creator walking in his creation. And as he touches the sick and breaks bread to feed the hungry, he is giving us a glimpse of the future. The Word of God is in the world remaking the world. When you read the stories of Jesus, you are seeing the future of creation. And what a glorious future it is…

### Meditate
*Through him all things were made;*
*without him nothing was made that*
*has been made.*

*At his Word the worlds were framèd;*
*He commanded; it was done:*
*Heaven and earth and depths of ocean*

*In their threefold order one;*
*All that grows beneath the shining*
*Of the moon and burning sun,*
*Evermore and evermore!*
*(Of the Father's Love Begotten)*

~~

## Prayer

*Lord Jesus Christ, we praise you.*
*You are the image of the invisible God,*
*the firstborn over all creation.*
*For in you all things were created:*
*things in heaven and on earth, visible and invisible,*
*whether thrones or powers or rulers or authorities;*
*all things have been created through you and for you.*
*You are before all things, and in you all things hold together.*

*And you are the head of the body, the church;*
*you are the beginning and the firstborn from among the dead,*
*so that in everything you might have the supremacy.*
*For God was pleased to have all his fullness dwell in you,*
*and through you to reconcile to himself all things,*
*whether things on earth or things in heaven,*
*by making peace through your blood, shed on the cross.*
*Amen.*

*(Adapted from Colossians 1 v 15-20)*

# Life

*"In him was life..."*
John 1 v 4

As I write this, I'm sitting at my desk at home. Every few minutes I get up to look out the window because I'm expecting the plumber. Our boiler made banging noises a couple of days ago and hasn't worked since. My deadline for this book is the end of the month, which is beginning to focus my mind. So I have to keep reminding myself that my aim as I write is not to pay the plumber or to avoid upsetting my publisher.

My aim is to convey something of the wonder of the incarnation. I want you to read the opening words of John's Gospel and feel excited, rather than simply informed.

I doubt John ever had problems with plumbers or publishers. But he, too, had an aim in mind when he wrote. He writes his Gospel, he tells us, so that, "you may believe that Jesus is the Messiah, the Son of God, and that by believing you may have life in his name" (20 v 31).

So John does not simply tell the story of the life, death and resurrection of Jesus. He also catalogues the promises of Jesus to give life:

- "For God so loved the world that he gave his one and only Son, that whoever believes in him shall not perish but have eternal life" (3 v 16).
- "You study the Scriptures diligently because you think that in them you have eternal life. These are the very Scriptures that testify about me, yet you refuse to come to me to have life" (5 v 39-40).
- "For the bread of God is the bread that comes down from heaven and gives life to the world" (6 v 33).
- "I am the living bread that came down from heaven. Whoever eats this bread will live for ever. This bread is my flesh, which I will give for the life of the world" (6 v 51).
- "The thief comes only to steal and kill and destroy; I have come that they may have life, and have it to the full" (10 v 10).
- "I give them eternal life, and they shall never perish; no one will snatch them out of my hand" (10 v 28).
- "I am the resurrection and the life. The one who believes in me will live, even though they die; and whoever lives by believing in me will never die" (11 v 25-26).
- "I am the way and the truth and the life" (14 v 6).

Jesus can give life because there is life in him. "In him was life." Theologians have a name for this: aseity. It literally means "from yourself".

My existence depends upon a lot of other things. It depends on my parents, who gave me birth. It depends on the farmers, manufacturers and retailers who produce my food. It depends on my employers, who pay me the money I need to buy that food. It depends on the water company that supplies clean water for me to drink. It depends on the medical services that keep me healthy. Above all it depends on God, who sustains all things and gives me each breath. I am not self-sufficient or self-sustaining. I do not have life in myself.

But Jesus says, "For as the Father has life in himself, so he has granted the Son also to have life in himself" (5 v 26).

Jesus does have life in himself. This is one of the things that marks Jesus out as truly divine. He is not a created being who depends on another for his existence.

∾

At the same time, mysteriously, Jesus has life in himself because the Father has given him life in himself. The Father is the source or origin of divinity. If this were not true, then there would be three divine Fathers.

But this gift of "life in himself" is an eternal gift. It's not that there was once a time when the Son didn't have life in himself. There wasn't a moment when the Father handed it over as a present to his Son—a gift with a before and after. The Son has always had life in himself. And that life has always been, and is always being, given to him by the Father.

This is why Jesus can give eternal life to his people. This is why Jesus can give eternal life to you. We are united to the eternally begotten Son. The Father is eternally giving life to the Son. And so, if we're in the Son by faith, the Father eternally gives life to us in and through the Son. Just as the Father continually gives life to the Son, so the Son continually gives life to his people in history, and will continue to do so beyond history into eternity.

The Son didn't simply hand over a gift-wrapped present of life to us on the day we became Christians. He gives us life day after day, hour after hour.

In this moment, as you read these words, if you believe in Jesus, he is giving you life—not merely the life of being alive as a person now, with a beating heart and a thinking brain, but the life of being alive as a person in relationship with God—life as it was designed by him to be experienced, and enjoyed, and continued eternally. In him is your life.

## Meditate

*In him was life…*

*When sin departs before his grace,*
*Then life and health come in its place.*
*Angels and men with joy may sing*
*All for to see the new-born King.*
(The Sussex Carol)

∽

## Prayer

*How priceless is your unfailing love, O God!*
*People take refuge in the shadow of your wings.*
*They feast in the abundance of your house;*
*you give them drink from your river of delights.*
*For with you is the fountain of life;*
*in your light we see light.*
*Continue your love to those who know you,*
*your righteousness to the upright in heart. Amen.*
(Psalm 36 v 7-10)

# Light

*"And that life was the light of all mankind."*
John 1 v 4

I usually wake up first in our house. Normally I thrash about in the dark, trying not to disturb my wife as I gather up my clothes before stumbling towards the bathroom. Only once I'm in the bathroom do I put on the light. And then all is clear. And usually, what is clear is that I've picked up the wrong clothes.

The first act of creation was the creation of light. "And God said, 'Let there be light,' and there was light" (Genesis 1 v 3). The world was in darkness. God spoke and there was light. God's word brought light to darkness.

Wherever and whenever God speaks, the result is light. "The unfolding of your words gives light" (Psalm 119 v 130). "For this command is a lamp, this teaching is a light, and correction and instruction are the way to life" (Proverbs 6 v 23). The opposite is also true. "If anyone does not speak according to this word, they have no light of dawn" (Isaiah 8 v 20). Where God's word is absent, darkness closes back in (Psalm 82 v 5; Ecclesiastes 2 v 13-14).

We know from our own experience how a word can bring light. Maybe there's a topic you find confusing. And then someone explains it clearly or comes up with a great illustration. And you say, "Ah, now I get it. Now it makes sense."

~

In a similar way humanity is confused about life, God, identity, truth and the future. We're confused because we're creatures with a limited understanding, and we're confused because we're sinners with a warped understanding.

But at the first Christmas, says John, God's Word was entering history in the person of Jesus. And what was the result? What it had always been and always is when God speaks: light. So John continues, "In him was life, and that life was the light of all mankind. The light shines in the darkness, and the darkness has not overcome it." John describes how John the Baptist came as a witness to the imminent coming of the light (v 6-8). "The true light that gives light to everyone was coming into the world" (v 9).

In the Old Testament God brings light through his Word. What John tells us is that Jesus is that Word, through whom God brings light.

And again that's what we see throughout John's Gospel. Jesus says, "I am the light of the world. Whoever follows me will never walk in darkness, but will have the light of life" (8 v 12).

In John 9, Jesus heals a blind man. It's a demonstration of his ability to bring light. The disciples assume the man must be blind because of some specific sin. So, since the man was born blind, they ask whether it was the sin of the man himself or his parents. But

Jesus says the man was born blind "so that the works of God might be displayed in him" (v 3). And what is it that will be displayed in this man? Jesus says, "While I am in the world, I am the light of the world" (v 5). By healing this man, Jesus is demonstrating that he is the light of the world.

When the Pharisees reject this healing and the healed man, Jesus comments, "For judgment I have come into this world, so that the blind will see and those who see will become blind" (v 39). This miracle embodies the way in which Jesus confirms the darkness of those who reject him, but brings light to those who receive him.

∾

The light God shines—the word he speaks—is Jesus. Now through the power of his Spirit, we're able to say, "Ah, now I get it. Now it makes sense." We're no longer blundering, no longer guessing. We can see the truth about life, God, identity, truth and the future. That is sometimes challenging—in the light of the Word, we see that we've picked up the wrong ideas or adopted the wrong behaviours. But that is always thrilling—because it brings clarity where once there was only confusion.

Jesus is the Word, through whom we hear God's voice and through whom God made the world. Now we see that Jesus is the Word through whom God brings light.

## Meditate

*And that life was the light of all mankind.*

*God of God, light of light,*
*Lo, he abhors not the Virgin's womb;*
*Very God, begotten, not created:*
*O come, let us adore him,*
*O come, let us adore him,*
*O come, let us adore him,*
*Christ the Lord.*
*(O Come, All Ye Faithful)*

∼

## Prayer

*O Christ, our Morning Star,*
*Splendour of Light Eternal,*
*shining with the glory of the rainbow,*
*come and waken us*
*from the greyness of our apathy,*
*and renew in us your gift of hope.*
*Amen.*
*(The Venerable Bede, 672-735)*

# Over7coming

*"The light shines in the darkness,
and the darkness has not overcome it."*
John 1 v 5

The darkness has not overcome the light, says John. Is that true? Is that how it feels in your neighbourhood? In your workplace? In your culture? Often it feels as if the darkness is overcoming. It feels as if the light is flickering and faltering, like a failing flame. "This is the verdict," says Jesus. "Light has come into the world, but people loved darkness instead of light because their deeds were evil" (3 v 19).

The darkness has not overcome the light, says John. Was that true at the cross? "Walk while you have the light," says Jesus, "before darkness overtakes you" (12 v 35). The word "overtake" is the same word as "overcome" here in 1 v 5. There was a moment when the darkness overcame the light. And that moment was the cross.

As Jesus hung on the cross, "darkness came over the whole land until three in the afternoon" (Mark 15 v 33). The light of the world was covered over by darkness. And then the light was extinguished.

The cross is the ultimate expression of human hatred of God. We constantly and consistently reject the light of God's revelation. Why? Because our deeds are evil. In other words, we don't want to face the reality of who we are. And we don't want to change who we are. We don't want to know God because we prefer evil. Romans 1 v 18-20 says that, "What may be known about God is plain to [people], because God has made it plain to them". But people "suppress the truth by their wickedness". We do this every day by ignoring the light of God. And when the light of God came in human form, we murdered him. Maybe now we can be left to our dark and evil ways.

But the light did not stay dead. "The light shines in the darkness, and the darkness has not overcome it." Jesus the light rose again at dawn on the third day. As the light of a new day broke, so the light of a new age dawned. "I have come into the world as a light," he said, "so that no one who believes in me should stay in darkness" (12 v 46).

∽

Here's the thing: light always wins. It's an unequal contest. We know this from our own experience. Light and darkness are asymmetrical. Light dispels darkness simply by its presence whereas darkness doesn't naturally extinguish light. You can't have a "torch-dark" that casts a beam of darkness into the light. But a "torch-light" casts a beam of light into the darkness—no matter how much darkness there is.

Jesus says, "Put your trust in the light while there is still time; then you will become children of the light" (12 v 36). If you have put your trust in Jesus the light, then you are a child of light. And the darkness has not and will not overcome the children of light.

The world does not stay in darkness. At Christmas light entered the world. At Christmas services we often read from Isaiah 9 v 2: "The people walking in darkness have seen a great light; on those living in the land of deep darkness a light has dawned."

With the coming of the Word, light broke into the darkness of this world; and with the resurrection of the Word, God declared that the light would never be extinguished. And, in putting our faith in Jesus, we have been called out of darkness. We need never be overcome by the darkness, and can always live in the light. There is never any need for, nor any excuse for, returning to the darkness.

## Meditate

*The light shines in the darkness,*
*and the darkness has not overcome it.*

*Hail the heav'n-born Prince of Peace!*
*Hail the Sun of Righteousness!*
*Light and life to all he brings,*
*Ris'n with healing in his wings.*
*Mild he lays his glory by,*
*Born that man no more may die.*
*Born to raise the sons of earth,*
*Born to give them second birth.*
*(Hark! The Herald Angels Sing)*

## Prayer

*Lord, you have given us your Word*
*for a light to shine upon our path.*
*Grant us so to meditate on that Word,*
*and to follow its teaching,*
*that we may find in it the light*
*that shines more and more*
*until the perfect day,*
*through Jesus Christ our Lord.*
*Amen.*

*(Jerome, c. 347-420)*

# Witness

*"There was a man sent from God whose
name was John.
He came as a witness to testify concerning
that light,
so that through him all might believe.
He himself was not the light;
he came only as a witness to the light."*
John 1 v 6-8

One Sunday I was talking to one of the mums in our congregation. I'd been preaching and she was thanking me for my sermon. Suddenly her four-year-old son piped up, "It's not all about you, Tim".

"It's not all about you" is one of the catchphrases we often use in our church. With every issue and in every situation, what really matters is God and his glory. It's a phrase we use to regain perspective. Presumably my young friend had picked up on this and was now ready to deploy it at will.

"There was a man sent by God" sounds at first like it could be introducing the Word-made-flesh. But, no: this man is someone else. And "It's not all about you"—or "It's not all about me"—

might well have been one of his catchphrases.

Verse 6 could be translated more literally as, "a man came from God whose name was John". The verb is the same as that used in verse 3, which is literally, "Through [the Word] all things came (into existence); without him nothing came (into existence) that has come (into existence)".

John came. But Jesus didn't come, at least, not in the same way. Instead, everything else came through Jesus—including John.

It's true that John came first in history. He was six months older than Jesus and he started his ministry before Jesus went public. But Jesus is the source of John just as Jesus is the source of everything that exists. This is how John himself puts it, saying, "He who comes after me has surpassed me because he was before me" (1 v 15, 30).

∽

We meet this idea of the superiority of Jesus in verses 7-8. John is a witness to the light. That's a tremendous privilege. John plays a key role in the history of the salvation. But Jesus is the light to whom John witnesses.

It may be that John the Evangelist (that is, the writer of the Gospel) had followers of John the Baptist in mind when he wrote these words (Acts 18 v 25; 19 v 3). Perhaps he wanted to persuade them that truly following John actually means following the one of whom John was a witness.

But it's also a reminder that, like John, we're secondary and Jesus is primary. "It's not all about you."

Just in case you think I'm doing John a disservice, this was his message. John himself said, "I baptise with water ... but among you stands one you do not know. He is the one who comes after me, the straps of whose sandals I am not worthy to untie" (1 v 26-27).

Later in this chapter, we read the story of two people who are John's "disciples" (v 35-39). What does John do with these disciples? He points them to Jesus so that they leave John and follow Jesus instead.

∽

We so easily become preoccupied with our own status. In situations of conflict, in social situations, in our careers, in our church meetings, we can make it all about us. We can manoeuvre to promote ourselves or contribute to further our interests. In these moments we need to tell ourselves, "Jesus must become greater; I must become less" (see John 3 v 30).

Personally, I don't shout and stamp my feet. That's not my style. Instead I go away and brood—although *sulk* might be a more accurate term. I feel misunderstood or mistreated. More times than I can count, I've got in a stew about a situation of conflict. And it makes me miserable. Every time, what sets me free is this thought: "It's not all about you, Tim. I must decrease that Jesus might increase." When this truth finally dawns on me, often the conflict suddenly doesn't seem to matter any more.

"Only a witness." That's how John is described in 1 v 8. And that's a good description of you and I. What makes us special is that we are witnesses to the light. John came "so that through him (John) all might believe (in Jesus)".

"Only" a witness—but gloriously, never less than a witness. May it be said of you that through your witness people have found life in the name of Jesus.

## Meditate

*He came as a witness to testify concerning that light,*
*so that through him all might believe.*
*He himself was not the light…*

*Come, thou long expected Jesus*
*Born to set thy people free;*
*From our fears and sins release us,*
*Let us find our rest in thee.*
*Israel's strength and consolation,*
*Hope of all the earth thou art;*
*Dear desire of every nation,*
*Joy of every longing heart.*
*(Come, Thou Long Expected Jesus)*

∽

## Prayer

*O Lord Jesus Christ,*
*who at your first coming sent your messenger*
*to prepare thy way before you:*
*Grant that the ministers and stewards of your mysteries*
*may likewise so prepare and make ready your way,*
*by turning the hearts of the disobedient to the wisdom of the just,*
*that at your second coming to judge the world*
*we may be found an acceptable people in your sight,*
*who lives and reigns with the Father and the Holy Spirit,*
*ever one God, world without end.*
*Amen.*
*(The Book of Common Prayer, the Collect*
*for the third Sunday in Advent)*

# Heaven opened

*"The true light that gives light to everyone
was coming into the world."*
John 1 v 9

Think of some of the fictional ways we've invented for moving between one realm and another: the rabbit hole in *Alice in Wonderland*, the Tardis in *Doctor Who*, the wardrobe in the *Narnia Chronicles*, a portkey in the Harry Potter books, the portal in the *Stargate* series. It seems we're obsessed with the idea of moving between dimensions. Perhaps that's because we were made to live at the intersection of heaven and earth, and so there are echoes of this all over our culture.

In verse 9, John speaks of light "coming into the world" from outside the world. If this were a sci-fi movie, we might imagine a beam of light connecting our world with another dimension.

Jesus uses a different image to describe this same intersection later in the chapter: "Very truly I tell you, you will see 'heaven open, and the angels of God ascending and descending on' the Son of Man" (1 v 51). He is pointing to a dream of Jacob, the father of the nation of Israel (Genesis 28 v 12-17). Jacob saw "the gate of heaven" with a stairway between heaven and earth. And now Jesus says, *I can lead you to the gate of heaven. I can show you the stairway to heaven.*

∼

Except that Jesus says much more than this. This is what Jacob sees in his dream: "A stairway resting on the earth, with its top reaching to heaven, and the angels of God were ascending and descending on it". The angels are ascending and descending on a stairway between heaven and earth.

Now look at what Jesus says in John 1 v 51: "You shall see heaven open, and the angels of God ascending and descending on the Son of Man". There's no mention of a stairway. The angels are ascending and descending on the Son of Man—on Jesus. Jesus is the stairway. He's the link between heaven and earth. He himself is the gate of heaven. He's the point at which heaven and earth intersect.

It's not that there's some secret ravine in the deserts of the Middle East with ancient inscriptions across the walls, and if you press the right spot or say the right words, then a gateway will open and the stairway to heaven will be revealed. This is not like Bilbo finding the secret doorway into Smaug's lair in the moonlight in Tolkien's *The Hobbit*, or Indiana Jones puzzling out some ancient code to reveal hidden treasure.

There is a link between heaven and earth. There is a portal. There is a gateway. And that gateway is Jesus. What Jacob saw in his dream was a picture—a picture of Jesus.

∼

Later in John's Gospel, Jesus says, "No one has ever gone into heaven" (3 v 13). But then he goes on… "except the one who came from heaven—the Son of Man". Jesus has stepped across the divide between heaven and earth. He's entered our world to be the bridge between heaven and earth.

This is what God said to Jacob in Jacob's dream: "I am with you and will watch over you wherever you go … I will not leave you until I have done what I have promised you" (Genesis 28 v 15). God shows Jacob the stairway between heaven and earth to reassure Jacob that he is with him and watches over him. Jesus is that stairway. And through Jesus, God is with us and God watches over us.

Think of the rabbit hole, the Tardis, the wardrobe, the portkey and the portal. The portal between heaven and earth is open right now and you can pass through it—because that portal is Jesus.

So don't let your eyes drop. It's all too easy for us just to see the horizons of this world and this life. And so we forget that we're linked with Christ in the heavenly realms. Live your life today as a citizen of heaven. Live as someone who is connected to the coming world. Live as someone to whom God says, "I am with you and I will watch over you wherever you go … I will not leave you until I have done what I have promised you."

*Tim Chester*

## Meditate

*You will see heaven open, and the angels of God ascending
and descending on the Son of Man.*

*And our eyes at last shall see him,
Through his own redeeming love,
For that child so dear and gentle
Is our Lord in heav'n above,
And he leads his children on
To the place where he is gone.
(Once In Royal David's City)*

∼

## Prayer

*Father God,
I thank you for the promise that
you are with me,
you will watch over me wherever I go,
and you will not leave me
until you have done what you have promised me.
Since I have been raised with Christ,
help me to set my heart on things above,
where Christ is seated at your right hand.
Amen.*

*(Based on Genesis 28 v 15 and Colossians 3 v 1)*

# Preferring darkness

*"He was in the world,
and though the world was made through him,
the world did not recognise him.
He came to that which was his own,
but his own did not receive him."*
John 1 v 10-11

I once woke up in the middle of the night to find a strange
figure at the foot of my bed. It was dark and I was half asleep,
so I couldn't work out who it was or what they were doing there.
Gradually the light dawned. It was my wetsuit, which I'd hung up
the night before.

In John 3 a man comes to Jesus at night and wonders why he
can't see! That man's name is Nicodemus. Nicodemus comes to Jesus
because he is concerned with spiritual insight, rather than physical
sight. But John plays on the fact that the meeting is taking place during
the darkness of night to highlight Nicodemus' real problem.

Nicodemus begins by suggesting Jesus must be from God (3
v 2). But behind this statement is a question: *Is Jesus God's promised
King? Is he the Messiah?*

If this were a world of light, it would be easy to see the truth
about Jesus. But this is a world in darkness, into which Jesus steps

as the true light (1 v 9). Verses 10-11 remind us of why we need light—because we live in darkness.

This means that to "see" God's kingdom—to understand its nature and welcome its coming—you need to be able to see in the dark. For that, you need help—you need the Spirit of God to make you a new person with new insight. Jesus says you need to be born again (3 v 3-8).

~୨

Then Jesus starts talking about snakes in the wilderness, which at first sight seems rather random (3 v 14)! He's asking Nicodemus to think of the episode told in Numbers 20. The people of Israel, on their way to the promised land, had rebelled against God, and so God had sent a plague of poisonous snakes as an act of judgment. The people repented, so God told Moses to make a bronze serpent and lift it high among the people. Anyone who looked to the serpent would be saved. Jesus says this was not only a means of rescue for those Israelites in that time—it was also a picture of what he would do at the cross: "Just as Moses lifted up the snake in the wilderness, so the Son of Man must be lifted up, that everyone who believes may have eternal life in him" (John 3 v 14-15).

Nicodemus asks whether Jesus is God's King. Jesus says you need God's Spirit to see God's King. Why? Because Jesus is not the King we expect. We expect a king to be high and mighty. Jesus would certainly be lifted up. But he would be lifted up on a cross.

And why is Jesus lifted up on a cross? Jesus continues, "For God so loved the world that he gave his one and only Son, that whoever believes in him shall not perish but have eternal life" (3 v 16). God's King would die in the place of his people. He had come not to defeat rebels, but to take their place—to be defeated by God so we can be forgiven.

∽

Finally, in his night-time conversation, Jesus comes back to the issue of darkness: "Light has come into the world, but people loved darkness instead of light because their deeds were evil" (3 v 19). People love darkness. They don't want to let go of their sin—they don't want to recognise the Word, and they don't want to receive their King (1 v 10-11). *Why?* Because people fear exposure. They don't want to admit their sin or give up their self-rule. Jesus is diagnosing what Nicodemus has done by coming furtively at night. Nicodemus is his own parable. He has come at night, asking, *"Why can't I see?"*

Jesus offers eternal life to rebellious subjects. But we prefer darkness and death to life in the light. We don't want to admit we need the King on the cross, dying for our sins. As a result, the cross looks like the epitome of shame to us rather than the epitome of glory. We call darkness light, and light darkness. We don't recognise the light that has come to us.

Only the Spirit of God can open our eyes to the true light. Only the Spirit of God can enable us to recognise and receive the truth of these words with joy: "The true light that gives light to everyone was coming into the world".

Tim Chester

## Meditate
*He was in the world,*
*and though the world was made through him,*
*the world did not recognise him.*

*Yet with the woes of sin and strife*
*The world has suffered long;*
*Beneath the angel strain have rolled*
*Two thousand years of wrong;*
*And man, at war with man, hears not*
*The love-song which they bring;*
*O hush the noise, ye men of strife*
*And hear the angels sing.*
*(It Came Upon the Midnight Clear)*

~

## Prayer
*Eternal God,*
*the light of the minds that know you,*
*the joy of the hearts that love you,*
*and the strength of the wills that serve you:*
*grant us so to know you that we may truly love you,*
*so to love you that we may truly serve you,*
*whose service is perfect freedom;*
*through Jesus Christ our Lord.*
*Amen.*
*(Augustine of Hippo, 354-430)*

# Children of God

11

*"Yet to all who did receive him,*
*to those who believed in his name,*
*he gave the right to become children of God."*
John 1 v 12

What does God think of you? God accepts you in Christ. You probably know that. But perhaps you think of God as tolerating you. At best, he puts up with your weaknesses, your sin and your ugliness for the sake of Christ. But his acceptance is reluctant—perhaps even begrudging.

John's view of God's view of us was nothing like this. "To those who believed in his name, he gave the right to become children of God." In his first letter, John says, "See what great love the Father has lavished on us, that we should be called children of God! And that is what we are!" (1 John 3 v 1). There's no sense here that Christ has twisted the arm of a reluctant God. Salvation begins with the Father's love. And his love is lavish. He has given us the right to become his children. 1 John 3 v 1 is literally, "See what kind of love the Father has given to us" or "See from what country the love of the Father has come". In other words, John is saying,

*Where did this love come from? It's like nothing we've ever seen before. It's literally out of this world.*

∽

John's first letter is in some ways an extended meditation on the idea he introduces here in verse 12 of the first chapter of his Gospel: God has given us the right to be his children. The letter begins with language that echoes John 1. The Word of life, which was in the beginning, has come in the flesh: "That which was from the beginning, which we have heard, which we have seen with our eyes, which we have looked at and our hands have touched—this we proclaim concerning the Word of life" (1 John 1 v 1).

But why has the Word come in the flesh? Why has John given his life to proclaiming the Word-made-flesh? "We proclaim to you what we have seen and heard, so that you also may have fellowship with us. And our fellowship is with the Father and with his Son, Jesus Christ. We write this to make our joy complete" (1 John 1 v 3-4).

We are in Christ and so we are in the Trinity. We are linked to the Son and so we are linked to the Trinity. We have become part of the triune community. We are part of the family.

So we share in the fellowship between the Father and the Son. God loves us with the same love that he has towards his own Son. God feels towards you the same that he feels towards Jesus. He can no more stop loving you than he can stop loving Jesus. John writes so his readers can experience joy (1 v 4)—the joy that comes from community with God!

John continues, "Everyone born of God overcomes the world. This is the victory that has overcome the world, even our faith.

Who is it that overcomes the world? Only the one who believes that Jesus is the Son of God" (1 John 5 v 4-5). Our job, as it were, is to believe that we are the children of God through the Son of God.

~

This is why Jesus came. This is what his advent, his arrival, is all about: giving us the right to become children of God. So our job is to live like his children so we become his children, just as my children have to live as I want them to in order to earn my love. Is that right?! Of course not. Just as humans are born as children with a father, so we Christians are born anew as children of our heavenly Father. Our new birth is what makes us God's children—not our efforts. Relating to God is not complicated or hard. It is as simple as a child relating to her father. So our job is to trust in God as our Father: to see his smile, to welcome his embrace, to enjoy his love.

## Meditate
*To those who believed in his name,*
*he gave the right to become children of God…*

*How silently, how silently, the wondrous gift is giv'n;*
*So God imparts to human hearts the blessings of his heav'n.*
*No ear may hear his coming, but in this world of sin,*
*Where meek souls will receive him still, the dear Christ enters in.*
*(O Little Town of Bethlehem)*

# Prayer

*Almighty God,*
*who has given us your only-begotten Son*
*to take our nature upon him,*
*and as at this time to be born of a pure Virgin:*
*Grant that we being regenerate,*
*and made your children by adoption and grace,*
*may daily be renewed by your Holy Spirit;*
*through the same our Lord Jesus Christ,*
*who lives and reigns with you*
*and the same Spirit,*
*ever one God, world without end.*
*Amen.*
*(The Book of Common Prayer, the*
*Collect for Christmas Day)*

# Born of God

*"Children born not of natural descent,*
*nor of human decision or a husband's will,*
*but born of God."*
John 1 v 13

My friend John was a merchant seaman who grew up without any knowledge of God. Then his father died, and that sent him into a spin. He and his wife started attending the church where she'd been to Sunday School as a child. John began to read his Bible.

One day he read John 5 v 24: "Very truly I tell you, whoever hears my word and believes him who sent me has eternal life and will not be judged but has crossed over from death to life". *That's me,* he thought. *I believe in Jesus so I must have crossed over from death to life.*

And do you know what John's first thought was? He was annoyed that God hadn't involved him in the decision. God had made him a Christian without consulting him first. He hadn't chosen God— God had chosen him. God had given him faith without him asking for it. John had been born again "not ... of human decision or a husband's will, but born of God".

The apostle Paul uses the idea of adoption to show that we are children of God. John uses the idea of rebirth. We are born again as children of God. And this is all of God. It's not based on human ability ("natural descent"). It's not based on human will ("human decision"). We believe in Christ's name (v 12) because we have first been born of God (v 13). "The wind blows wherever it pleases. You hear its sound, but you cannot tell where it comes from or where it is going. So it is with everyone born of the Spirit" (3 v 8).

Our role is to believe in Jesus and believe we have become children of God through him. And with this, everything else falls into place. As John reflects in his first letter on what it means to be born of God, he shows how it transforms our lives:

- **Being children of God transforms our behaviour.** "No one who is born of God will continue to sin, because God's seed remains in them; they cannot go on sinning, because they have been born of God" (1 John 3 v 9). God's DNA is in us. So we're being changed into the family likeness until eventually we become like him (3 v 2-3).

- **Being children of God transforms our relationships.** "Dear friends, let us love one another, for love comes from God. Everyone who loves has been born of God and knows God" (1 John 4 v 7). Other Christians are also God's children, and so they're our brothers and sisters. We love our church family with the love we've received.

- **Being children of God transforms our fears.** "There is no fear in love. But perfect love drives out fear, because fear has to do with punishment" (1 John 4 v 18). We don't fear judgment because, in his love, God has dealt with our judgment on the cross (v 10).

- **Being children of God transforms our prayers.** "This

is the confidence we have in approaching God: that if we ask anything according to his will, he hears us" (1 John 5 v 14). Just as a human father delights to hear the faltering words of his child, so our heavenly Father delights to hear our faltering prayers.

- ⌁ **Being children of God transforms our future.** "We know that anyone born of God does not continue to sin; the One who was born of God keeps them safe, and the evil one cannot harm them" (1 John 5 v 18). God may allow bad things to happen, but never more than we can bear and always to make us more like his Son. Nothing and no one can remove us from the family.

But always remember: we don't start with changed behaviour, relationships, fears or prayers. We start by believing we're the children of God through the Son of God. This is what changes everything else.

~

In CS Lewis's *The Chronicles of Narnia*, the central characters enter another world in which they are sons of Adam and daughters of Eve. They inherit humanity's true identity as kings and queens in God's world. But back in this world, the children are bullied for their claim to be royal. Or they're mocked by their cousin, Eustace. Yet as soon as they arrive in Narnia, the Narnians bow before them, recognising them as kings and queens of Narnia.

It's a picture of our status as children of God. "The people who belong to this world don't recognise that we are God's children because they don't know him" (1 John 3 v 10, *New Living Translation*). This world doesn't know God, and so it doesn't understand that we're his children. But we really are! We're sons and daughters of God, made and remade to reign with God.

The advent of Jesus changes our lives because it changes our status. Jesus makes us children of God. It was his choice, for we would never have made that choice. And it was a wonderful choice—one that we will increasingly appreciate, and thank him for, eternally.

## Meditate

*See what great love the Father has lavished on us, that we should be called children of God! And that is what we are!*

*O holy child of Bethlehem, descend to us, we pray;*
*Cast out our sin, and enter in, be born in us today.*
*We hear the Christmas angels the great glad tidings tell;*
*O come to us, abide with us, our Lord Emmanuel!*
*(O Little Town of Bethlehem)*

∼

## Prayer

*Father God,*
*may I know that I'm your child.*
*And may knowing that I'm your child:*
*transform my behaviour as I adopt your likeness,*
*transform my relationships as I love your family,*
*transform my fears as I embrace your love,*
*transform my prayers as I accept your welcome,*
*transform my future as I trust your care.*
*Amen.*

# God in a manger

*"The Word became flesh..."*
John 1 v 14

Imagine you're away from your loved ones. What do you do? You text them. You try to phone them. You send them a letter. If you can't be physically present with someone, then you try to be present with them through your words. That phone call expresses something of your love and commitment. Even if you have nothing significant to say, you discuss the trivialities of your day because you want to hear their voice.

In Jesus, the Word of God comes to us. We hear the voice of God expressing his love and commitment to us.

But this Word is a Word made flesh. God the Father doesn't just phone us. His Word is made flesh. His Word is physically present. It is a Word that John has heard and seen and touched (1 John 1 v 1-3).

God takes on flesh. God lies in a manger. God plays with other children. God eats round the table. God sweats on the roadside. God sleeps in the boat. God shares our human weakness. God experiences our temptations.

This is the wonder of the incarnation. God is clothed in human flesh: "For in Christ all the fullness of the Deity lives in bodily form" (Colossians 2 v 9). It's as if the splendour of God has been squeezed into a human body. Imagine trying to pack all your possessions into a suitcase—squashing it, pushing it, sitting on it, trying to cram them all in. That is what God did at the incarnation. He took the fullness of the Deity and squeezed it into bodily form. And nothing was left out. Jesus is truly divine and truly human. Christmas marks the coming of God.

∽

It's this truth that is beautifully captured in one of the oldest and most widely acknowledged creeds in the Christian church: the Nicene Creed. It began life at the Council of Nicea in AD 325 and is thought to have been revised at the Council of Constantinople in AD 381. This is what it says about the person of Jesus:

> We believe in one Lord, Jesus Christ,
> the only Son of God,
> eternally begotten of the Father,
> God from God,
> Light from Light,
> true God from true God,
> begotten, not made,
> of one Being with the Father.

Making this affirmation matters because it means we can know with confidence what God is like. "No one has ever seen God, but the one and only Son, who is himself God and is in the closest relationship with the Father, has made him known" (John 1 v 18).

God is unseen and unseeable—except in Jesus, who makes him known. And he makes him known truly because he himself is God.

What is God really like? Look at Jesus. He is the perfect image of God. And in Jesus we see a God who has entered into the pain and confusion of human history to reconcile us to himself.

Christianity is not a call to embrace a system of thought or a religion or a moral code. It's the invitation to embrace a person— or rather to be embraced by a person. It's the invitation to look to Jesus and see in him the kindness, glory, beauty, power and holiness of God.

The Word became flesh. Wisdom became flesh. Love became flesh. Holiness became flesh. Justice became flesh. Truth became flesh. And his name is Jesus.

## Meditate
*The Word became flesh…*

*He came down to earth from heaven,*
*Who is God and Lord of all,*
*And his shelter was a stable,*
*And his cradle was a stall;*
*With the poor, and mean, and lowly,*
*Lived on earth our Saviour holy.*

*For he is our childhood's pattern;*
*Day by day, like us he grew;*
*He was little, weak and helpless,*
*Tears and smiles like us he knew;*
*And he feeleth for our sadness,*
*And he shareth in our gladness.*
*(Once in Royal David's City)*

## Prayer
*O Lord God,*
*thou hast commanded me to believe in Jesus;*
*and I would flee to no other refuge,*
*wash in no other fountain,*
*build on no other foundation,*
*receive from no other fullness,*
*rest in no other relief.*
*Amen.*

*(From "Jesus my Glory" in The Valley of Vision)*

# God's new address

**14**

*"The Word became flesh*
*and made his dwelling among us."*
John 1 v 14

One of my friends lives in Epsom in Surrey. In 2007, Chelsea Football Club officially opened new training facilities nearby. Since then members of the team and staff have moved into the neighbourhood. As a result local house prices have risen, because the area has become a more desirable place to live in. Chelsea FC have added value to the neighbourhood.

When the Word became flesh, Jesus moved into our neighbourhood. He "made his dwelling among us". The word "dwelling" is literally "tabernacled". Jesus the Word tabernacled among us. In Jesus, God pitched his tent among us.

～

John is pointing us to the story of Israel in the desert after God had liberated them from slavery in Egypt. God told Moses to build a tent or tabernacle in which God would live among his people.

Constructing a tent for God might seem to us an odd thing to do. Perhaps we start thinking of a wedding marquee or a camping trip. But to the Israelites at that time, a tent meant only one thing: home. They lived in tents. And now God was moving into the neighbourhood. He was going to dwell among his people. He would live in a tent among the tents of his people—"Then let them make a sanctuary for me, and I will dwell among them" (Exodus 25 v 8).

The tabernacle was a sign of God's presence. Now, John announces, that sign has given way to the reality. God himself is dwelling among us in the person of Jesus. Jesus is God making his home among us. Jesus is, as it were, God's address on earth.

Whenever the Israelites pitched camp, the tabernacle was at the centre of the camp. It was a physical sign that God was among his people.

Imagine a young boy walking down the road. Suddenly, he sees the school bully coming towards him. What does he feel? If he's on his own, then he feels a shiver down his spine and sweat on his brow—and for good reason. But suppose he looks over his shoulder and there's his father walking behind him. That makes all the difference. Then there is no fear.

When Israel looked up and saw the tabernacle in the middle of the camp, they knew they were safe. God was with them and he would protect them. And we, too, can look up and "see" Jesus, who walked on this earth and who works on this earth by his Spirit. God is present among us to deliver us and protect us.

Or think of the moment in *The Lord of the Rings* when the battle for Helm's Deep looks lost. In that moment Aragorn remembers the words of Gandalf: "Look to my coming, at first light, on the fifth day. At dawn, look to the east." So he looks to the east and on the brow of the hill he sees Gandalf, along with the once-exiled riders of Rohan. He sees deliverance. He sees hope.

In our moments of despair when all hope looks lost, we can look to the east. We can look to Jesus. And we can know that God is for us. God is among us. God will deliver us.

## Meditate
*The Word became flesh and tabernacled among us.*

*Shepherds, in the fields abiding,*
*Watching o'er your flocks by night,*
*God with us is now residing,*
*Yonder shines the infant light:*
*Come and worship, come and worship*
*Worship Christ, the newborn King.*
*(Angels from the Realms of Glory)*

~

## Prayer
*O Thou, whose glorious, yet contracted light,*
*Wrapt in night's mantle, stole into a manger;*
*Since my dark soul, and brutish, is thy right,*
*To Man of all beast be not thou a stranger.*
*Furnish & deck my soul, that thou mayest have*
*A better lodging, than a rack or grave.*
*(From "Christmas" by George Herbert, 1593-1633)*

# The glory of God

*"We have seen his glory..."*
John 1 v 14

I recently witnessed a partial eclipse of the sun. Every piece of coverage on the news warned us not to look directly at the sun. I wondered about making a pin-hole viewer out of an old box. But in the event there was thin cloud—thin enough for the sun to be seen, but thick enough to enable us to look at the eclipse safely. What I did not do is ignore the warnings. If you look directly at the sun as it shines, it will damage your eyes.

In verse 14, John mentions a word we often say in Christian circles, but about which we rarely stop to think what we mean: glory. Literally, glory means "weight"—the heaviness of something, the nature of it. God's glory is God's God-ness. And looking at the glory of God can damage more than your eyes. God's glory comes with a health warning.

We've seen how God-made-flesh "tabernacled" among us in the person of his Son. We've seen that this was an echo and fulfilment of the tabernacle in the wilderness.

This is what happened when the first tabernacle was first erected: "The cloud covered the tent of meeting, and the glory of the LORD filled the tabernacle. Moses could not enter the tent of meeting because the cloud had settled on it, and the glory of the LORD filled the tabernacle" (Exodus 40 v 34-35). The presence of God means the glory of God. The glory of God descended on the tabernacle and Moses was forced to evacuate. Twice the text says that "the glory of the LORD filled the tabernacle".

This has happened again, and fully, in Jesus. "We have seen his glory." God has pitched his tabernacle among us in the person of Jesus. And God has filled his tabernacle with his glory. We see the glory of God in the person of his Son.

∽

In Exodus 33 v 18, Moses says to God, "Now show me your glory". It's a bold request. And God responds graciously and generously. But there's a problem. God will reveal his glory in his name. "'But,' he said, 'you cannot see my face, for no one may see me and live'" (v 20). So Moses can only be near God's glory, but he cannot see it: "When my glory passes by, I will put you in a cleft in the rock and cover you with my hand until I have passed by. Then I will remove my hand and you will see my back; but my face must not be seen" (v 22-23). On Mount Sinai, God will pass by and Moses will see the afterglow of his glory.

Hundreds of years later, another prophet is at Mount Sinai (or Mount Horeb as it was also known). Elijah is weary and disillusioned. So God says to him, "Go out and stand on the mountain in the presence of the LORD, for the LORD is about to pass by" (1 Kings 19 v 11). Again God passes by. He passes by to reveal his glory.

~

Hundreds of years later, the disciples are straining at the oars of their boat. The wind is against them, and they're getting nowhere. Jesus is praying on a mountain. But when he sees them straining, he goes out to them, walking on the water across the lake.

Mark tells us that "he was about to pass by them" (Mark 6 v 48). At first sight that seems a really odd thing to do. Jesus sees his friends in trouble, goes out to them and then seems to ignore them. Has he lost interest?

We need to read this story alongside the stories of Moses and Elijah. In those stories God passed by to reveal his glory. And now God in Jesus again passes by to reveal his glory.

But here's the difference: Jesus isn't on the mountain. He's left the mountain to go out to his disciples. And then he climbs into the boat (6 v 51).

The God of glory is in the boat with his friends—with us. In the place where we are straining, God is with us to reveal his glory.

"We're all in the same boat," we sometimes say to one another. In other words, we face the same problem. Jesus says to us, *We're in the same boat*. The problem you face, you don't face alone. Jesus is with you.

"We have seen his glory," says John. I think you can detect the wonder he still feels at this, decades later. God had told Moses, "You cannot see my face, for no one may see me and live". John has looked into the face of Jesus and has seen the glory of God. And he's lived to tell the tale.

## Meditate
*We have seen his glory...*

*O come, Adonai, Lord of might,*
*Who to thy tribes, on Sinai's height,*
*In ancient times didst give the law*
*In cloud and majesty and awe.*
*Rejoice! Rejoice! Emmanuel*
*Shall come to thee, O Israel.*
*(O Come, O Come Emmanuel)*

~

## Prayer
*Lord Jesus,*
*come to me now in your goodness.*
*Come to spread your treasures,*
*to enrich my heart with all grace and strength,*
*to bear all afflictions,*
*to encounter all dangers,*
*to bring peace of conscience,*
*and joy in the Holy Spirit.*
*Come to make my heart, as it were, a heaven.*
*Empty your goodness into my soul.*
*Amen.*

*(Adapted from "Bowels Opened"*
*by Richard Sibbes, 1577–1635)*

# The duty of
# enjoying glory

*"We have seen his glory..."*
John 1 v 14

I'm handing this chapter over to a guest writer. It's another John—
the seventeenth century English Puritan, John Owen (1616–
1683). John Owen wrote a book entitled *The Glory of Christ*. "We
have seen his glory," says the first-century John. So the seventeenth-
century John exhorts us to behold the glory of Christ—to look at,
think about, focus on and feel differently because of who we see
God to be in the Word-become-flesh:

> Let us regard it as our duty to meditate frequently on his
> glory. It is the neglect of meditation that keeps so many
> Christians in a feeble state.
>
> On Christ's glory I would fix all my thoughts and
> desires, and the more I see of the glory of Christ, the more
> the painted beauties of this world will wither in my eyes
> and I will be more and more crucified to this world.

Some talk much of imitating Christ and following his example. But no man will ever become "like him" by trying to imitate his behaviour and life if they knew nothing of the transforming power of beholding his glory.

Make up your mind that to behold the glory of God by beholding the glory of Christ is the greatest privilege which is given to believers in this life. This is the dawning of heaven. It is the first taste of that heavenly glory which God has prepared for us, for "this is eternal life, to know the Father and Jesus Christ whom he has sent" (John 17 v 3).

It is by beholding the glory of Christ by faith that we are spiritually edified and built up in this world, for as we behold his glory, the life and power of faith grow stronger and stronger. It is by faith that we grow to love Christ. So if we desire strong faith and powerful love, which give us rest, peace and satisfaction, we must seek them by diligently beholding the glory of Christ by faith. In this duty I desire to live and to die.

A constant view of the glory of Christ will revive our souls and cause our spiritual lives to flourish and thrive. Our souls will be revived by the transforming power with which beholding Christ is always accompanied. This is what transforms us daily into the likeness of Christ. So let us live in constant contemplation of the glory of Christ, and power will then flow from him to us, healing all our declensions (failings), renewing a right spirit in us and enabling us to abound in all the duties that God requires of us.

~

Follow Owen's advice as you read the stories of Jesus in the Gospels, as you read the promises and pictures of Jesus in the Old Testament, and as you read the explanation of Jesus in the New Testament. Think in terms of beholding the glory of Christ. Make it your habit to read the Bible in this way. Think how what you're reading reveals the character of Jesus or how it reveals the work of Jesus.

Imagine that the passage is placing Jesus on a stand for you to admire. What do you see? What is it that's admirable? How does Jesus reveal the glory of God? That is how you can see God's glory, even though, unlike the first-century John, you can't touch him—yet.

### Meditate

*The glory of the one and only Son … full of grace and truth.*

*Born thy people to deliver,*
*Born a child and yet a King,*
*Born to reign in us forever,*
*Now thy gracious kingdom bring.*
*By thine own eternal Spirit*
*Rule in all our hearts alone;*
*By thine all sufficient merit,*
*Raise us to thy glorious throne.*
*(Come, Thou Long Expected Jesus)*

## Prayer

*Father God,*
*help me to fix all my thoughts and desires*
*on the glory of Christ,*
*for this is my greatest privilege;*
*this is the dawning of heaven.*
*May beholding the glory of Christ*
*revive my soul,*
*heal my failings,*
*renew my spirit,*
*transforming me daily into the likeness of Christ,*
*and enabling me to abound*
*in all the duties that you require of me.*
*Amen.*

# The perfections of God

*"The glory of the one and only Son,*
*who came from the Father,*
*full of grace and truth."*
John 1 v 14

In the centre of Sheffield where I live is a fountain. Its surface is flat, continuous with the walk-way around it. But set in the surface are 89 individual jets of water. Sometimes they're set to pulse at irregular intervals. In the summer people run between them. And inevitably they end up soaking wet.

John is inviting us to be soaked by God's glory. And the fountain is Jesus.

In Exodus 33 Moses asks to see God's glory. But God cannot reveal his face for no one may see him and live. Instead God will reveal his name (33 v 19).

This is what happens: "Then the LORD came down in the cloud and stood there with him and proclaimed his name, the LORD. And he passed in front of Moses, proclaiming, 'The LORD, the LORD, the compassionate and gracious God, slow to anger, abounding in love and faithfulness'" (Exodus 34 v 5-6). The word "love" is the word for "covenant mercy". It's an expression of God's grace. And the word "faithfulness" is the word "truth". God is true to his promises.

It seems that this is what John has in mind when he speaks of God's glory being "full of grace and truth". The glory of God, full of grace—undeserved, lavish kindness—and truth—complete, life-guiding clarity—is seen in Jesus. Jesus is "the one and only". There is no one like him.

∽

God's glory is often associated in the Old Testament with light (Psalm 29 v 2; 96 v 8-9). God's glory is God's perfections radiating out of him like light radiating out of the sun. That glory streams into the person of his Son and radiates out from him so that God's glory is seen in the world. Imagine the Father pouring his glory into his Son like water into a pot. Then that glory overflows like a fountain out into the world. The closer you are to Jesus, the wetter you get.

Jesus reflects the Father's glory to perfection for he is the perfect image of God. The light of God's glory is perfectly reflected in the image or mirror of his Son. The Father sees in his Son a perfect reflection of his perfections. And so in this way the Son shares the Father's glory. From all eternity God's perfections pour out from the Father to the Son and back to the Father through the Spirit.

Think for a moment of some of the ways in which Jesus reflects the perfections of God. We see in Jesus the perfection of God's mercy. Without ever ignoring or downplaying the seriousness of sin, Jesus offers free forgiveness. As the nails are being driven into his hands, he prays, "Father forgive them" (Luke 23 v 34).

We see in Jesus the perfection of God's holiness. Think of the provocations he faced: the slowness of the disciples, the hatred of the religious leaders, the betrayal of his friends, the fickleness of the crowd, the injustice of Pilate, the cruelty of the soldiers. He was "tempted in every way ... yet he did not sin" (Hebrews 4 v 15).

We see in Jesus the perfection of God's power. Waves obeyed him. Sickness obeyed him. Demons obeyed him. Even death obeyed him.

We see in Jesus the perfection of God's wisdom. When the religious leaders tried to trick him, he turned their intrigue back on them so they condemned themselves. Yet his words also bring wholeness and health to our lives.

On and on we could go. I encourage you to get in the habit of reading Gospels to see the glory of Christ in the story of Christ— to behold, and soak in, and enjoy his grace and his truth. With every story, every saying, every encounter, ask yourself, "How do I see the glory of Christ in this?"

Above all we see in Jesus the perfection of God's love. John often speaks of Jesus being "lifted up" (3 v 14; 8 v 28; 12 v 32, 34). Jesus said, "And I, when I am lifted up from the earth, will draw all people to myself". And then John adds, "He said this to show the kind of death he was going to die" (12 v 32-33). At the climax of his life, Jesus is lifted up—like a king. But he is lifted up on a cross, as a criminal. His throne is the cross and his dais is the hill of Calvary. And this is his glory. It is the glory of love.

## Meditate

*Glory ... full of grace and truth.*

*He rules the world with truth and grace,*
*And makes the nations prove*
*The glories of his righteousness,*
*And wonders of his love,*

*And wonders of his love,*
*And wonders, wonders, of his love.*
*(Joy to the World)*

~

## Prayer
*Lord God,*
*you are full of wisdom, goodness,*
*righteousness, tenderness and compassion,*
*clothed with unchangeable perfections,*
*the origin of the goodness in any creature,*
*the author of the beauty of the world.*

*Lord Jesus, Redeemer,*
*you descended from the throne of majesty*
*to the vale of misery,*
*took our flesh when you had no need of it,*
*stooped to the infirmities of our nature,*
*for no other design than a thirst for our welfare,*
*carried yourself with all sweetness and tenderness in the world,*
*the exact image of your Father.*
*For this we give you love and praise.*
*Amen.*

*(Adapted from "A Discourse on the Knowledge of God"*
*by Stephen Charnock, 1628–1680)*

# God's native language

*"John testified concerning him.*
*He cried out, saying,*
*'This is the one I spoke about when I said,*
*"He who comes after me has surpassed me*
*because he was before me."'"*
John 1 v 15

It's a good rule of thumb not to ask questions to which you won't be able to understand the answer. I once asked someone, "Where in Kazakhstan are you from?" As soon as I said it, I realised there was no answer to that question that would mean anything to me. They told me they were from Emba—and of course, I was none the wiser. A more sensible question for me to have asked would have been, "Where's Kazakhstan?"

In a similar way, there's no answer to the question "What is God like?" that we could comprehend. There's no shared point of reference. You might as well ask what lies beyond the universe or what's in a fifth dimension.

Except for Jesus. Jesus is the shared point of reference. Jesus is God making himself known.

John the Baptist was the last and greatest prophet—bringer of a divine message—of the Old Covenant. But John the Baptist says that Jesus surpasses him. John the Baptist is a great prophet. But Jesus is the greater prophet: the ultimate prophet.

Jesus is the ultimate prophet not simply because he brings better word. Jesus is the greatest prophet because he himself is the message. He doesn't simply pass on a message from God like every other prophet. He himself is the message.

∾

The letter of Hebrews begins, "In the past God spoke to our ancestors through the prophets at many times and in various ways, but in these last days he has spoken to us by his Son" (Hebrews 1 v 1-2). There's no definite article or pronoun with the word "Son" in the original. It's not "in the Son" or "by his Son". It's literally "in Son". God speaks in Son just as I speak in English.

Recently I was preaching in Italy. I only speak English; the congregation spoke Italian, so someone had to translate. What language does God speak? My Welsh friends like to joke that Welsh is the language of heaven—but the letter of Hebrews says that God's native language is "Son". God translated himself into Hebrew and Greek when he spoke through the prophets and apostles, but his native tongue is his Son.

Jesus is the Word through whom God reveals himself in himself. Jesus is the Word who is God. Jesus is not just a very good prophet. Jesus is God and therefore he perfectly reveals God.

∾

But it's not, I think, just that Jesus is God. The Father revealed himself in the Bible, but the Father is not the Word of God. The Spirit inspired the Bible, but the Spirit is not the Word of God. Only

Jesus is the Word of God. Jesus is the Person of the Trinity through whom the Trinity reveals itself. It could be that, apart from Jesus, God is silent. If you took away my words, then I couldn't speak. If you took away Jesus-the-Word, then God couldn't communicate. God's revelation in creation, in history and in Scripture are all mediated through the Son. Creation is *made* through the Son, God *acts in history* through his Son and Scripture is *the record of God's revelation* in his Son.

So it's not just that Jesus is a better prophet with better access to God and a better word from God—though all of that is true. The point is there are no other prophets apart from Jesus. The word the prophets heard from God and passed on to their hearers was Jesus. The person they saw in their visions was Jesus. The angel of the LORD they encountered was Jesus. The word you read in the Bible is Jesus.

When you grasp this, you love him all the more, and you read him in his word all the more, and you appreciate the privilege of knowing God through him all the more.

## Meditate

*In the past God spoke to our forefathers through the prophets*
*at many times and in various ways,*
*but in these last days he has spoken to us in Son.*

*See amid the winter's snow,*
*Born for us on earth below,*
*See the tender Lamb appears,*
*Promised from eternal years.*

*Hail, thou ever-blessed morn!*
*Hail, redemption's happy dawn!*
*Sing through all Jerusalem,*
*Christ is born in Bethlehem.*
*(See Amid the Winter's Snow)*

## Prayer

*Break Thou the bread of life, dear Lord, to me,*
*as Thou didst break the bread beside the sea.*
*Beyond the sacred page I seek Thee, Lord.*
*My spirit pants for Thee, O living Word!*

*Thou art the bread of life, O Lord, to me.*
*Thy holy Word the truth that saveth me.*
*Give me to eat and live with Thee above.*
*Teach me to love Thy truth, for Thou art love.*

*O send Thy Spirit, Lord, now unto me,*
*that He may touch my eyes, and make me see.*
*Show me the truth concealed within Thy Word,*
*and in Thy Book revealed I see Thee, Lord.*

*(Adapted from "Break Thou the Bread of Life"*
*verses 1-2 by Mary Lathbury, 1841-1913, and verse 3*
*by Alexander Groves, 1842-1909)*

# The way home

19

*"Out of his fullness we have all received grace
in place of grace already given."*
John 1 v 16

I recently caught the bus to Matlock and then walked back to my home in Sheffield through the Peak District National Park. It's a 20-mile journey, and I'm not a young man any more, so I was relieved to see the *Welcome to Sheffield* sign on the outskirts of the city. It was good to see that sign. But the reality of getting home to a hot bath was even better.

"Grace already given." That's a reference to the law of Moses (as verse 17 will make clear). The giving of the law was an act of grace. It revealed God's will, highlighted our need, and pictured God's ultimate provision in Jesus Christ. It was a wonderful sign.

But the law itself couldn't save us. It could only reveal our need of salvation, and point to our Saviour. That's why John says, "Out of his fullness we have all received grace in the place of grace already given". Jesus has added grace to grace. The law was an act of grace, but only because it pointed to the true grace to come in Jesus. The sign was good. The reality is far better.

～

There are many ways in which Jesus brings grace in place of grace by fulfilling the promises embodied in the law. But what John has just been talking about is Jesus dwelling, or "tabernacling" among us (v 14). Jesus fulfils what was pictured in the tabernacle.

God placed the first man and woman in the garden-home of Eden. We were at home with God. But when we rejected God, we were exiled from Eden. Ever since, whether or not we've ever realised it or thought of it this way, we've all had a deep longing for home.

It was to address this sense of dislocation that God provided the plan for the tabernacle in Exodus 25 – 27. The tabernacle was a map showing us the way back home. So it was full of echoes of Eden. The clues were all embedded in the architecture and furnishings. The lampstand, for example, was covered in buds and blossoms (Exodus 25 v 31-36). The tabernacle looked like a garden with a tree that gave light. It was an echo of the tree of life at the centre of Eden. Seven times in the account of creation in Genesis 1 we read, "God said" (Genesis 1 v 3, 6, 9, 14, 20, 24, 26). And seven times in the tabernacle instructions we read, "The LORD said to Moses" (Exodus 25 v 1; 30 v 11, 17, 22, 34; 31 v 1, 12). Moreover, both accounts culminate in a description of the Sabbath (Genesis 2 v 1-3; Exodus 31 v 12-18). The building of the tabernacle was a symbolic rebuilding of our garden-home in Eden.

So the tabernacle was an echo back to Eden and a pointer forward to our true home. And what is our true home like? Again, the clues are embedded in the furniture of the tabernacle.

- ◆ **The ark was designed as the footstool of a king** (Exodus 25 v 10-22). This was where God would meet with his people to give them his commands. Home is the place where we live under the reign of God.

- ◆ **The table had the bread of the Presence on it at all times** (v 23-30). It wasn't there because God was hungry—rather, it was a permanent sign that God invites us to enjoy community with him. Home is the place where we eat in the presence of God.

- ◆ **The lamp looked like a life-giving tree, but it was also a light-giving lamp** (v 31-40). So God's prototype of home was a place of both life and light. Home is the place where we walk in the light of God.

If these were signposts showing us the way home, where did they point? The answer is given in verse 14: "The Word became flesh and made his dwelling among us". Jesus "tabernacled" among us. God made his home among us in the person of Jesus. Jesus is the point where heaven touches earth:

- ◆ **Jesus is the true ark.** He is the place (or the person) where we live under the reign of God. He is the King through whom God reigns.

- ◆ **Jesus is the true bread.** He is the bread through whom we eat in the presence of God. He said, "I am the bread of life. Whoever comes to me will never go hungry" (John 6 v 35).

- ◆ **Jesus is the true lamp.** He is the light of God, in whom we walk. He said, "I am the light of the world. Whoever follows me will never walk in darkness, but will have the light of life" (John 8 v 12).

"We have all received grace in place of grace already given"—

grace upon grace… grace and then more grace. Today, enjoy this grace upon grace. Not the grace of a footstool behind a curtain, but the grace upon grace of the living King, who reigns on behalf of his people. Not the grace of bread on a table, but the grace upon grace of the living Bread, who brings true satisfaction and joy. Not the grace of a lamp on a stand, but the living Light, who reveals the living God. What grace we have received!

## Meditate
*We have all received grace in place of grace already given.*

> *For lo! the days are hastening on,*
> *By prophet-bards foretold,*
> *When with the ever circling years*
> *Comes round the age of gold;*
> *When peace shall over all the earth*
> *Its ancient splendors fling,*
> *And the whole world send back the song*
> *Which now the angels sing.*
> *(It Came Upon the Midnight Clear)*

## Prayer
*Father God, I thank you for Jesus, the true ark:*
*may I live gladly under his reign today.*
*I thank you for Jesus, the true bread:*
*may I find satisfaction in him today.*
*I thank you for Jesus, the true lamp:*
*may I walk in the light of his gospel today. Amen.*

# Radiating glory

*"For the law was given through Moses;*
*grace and truth came through Jesus Christ."*
John 1 v 17

I like to think I have a stare that can quell small children. If they're misbehaving, I give them my "cross look". If that doesn't work then I move to Step Two—my "cross voice". Don't tell any children this, but I have to hope that between them my cross look and my cross voice will do the trick because I don't have a Step Three. Moses, however, really did have a look that put the fear of God in people.

When Moses came down from Mount Sinai, "his face was radiant because he had spoken with the LORD" (Exodus 34 v 29)—so much so that people were afraid to come near him. Moses encountered the glory of God, and as result he radiated with the reflected glory of God. So Moses had to wear a veil over his face when he was among the people, only taking it off when he went into God's presence.

The fear of the people at the radiant face of Moses was a picture of the impact of the law of God. The law is good, for it reflects the will and character of God. But still it brings fear. After God spoke the Ten Commandments, the Israelites "trembled with fear" and "remained at a distance" (Exodus 20 v 18-21). The law brings fear because it reveals God's holiness and exposes our sin. We feel the great gap between us and God, and instinctively shrink from him.

But "grace and truth came through Jesus Christ". Jesus bridges the gap. The law set the standard. It was a good standard, but a standard we could never meet. Jesus meets the standard on our behalf. He perfectly or righteously fulfils the law. He is the truth. And in his grace, his "righteousness" (his rightness before God) becomes our righteousness, if we are in him by faith. We no longer need to tremble at a distance. Jesus removes our fear and brings us near.

∽

In 2 Corinthians 3 – 4, Paul reflects on this story of Moses radiating the glory of God. He says that Christians radiate God's glory like Moses. With "unveiled faces", we "contemplate the Lord's glory". As a result, we "are being transformed into his image with ever-increasing glory, which comes from the Lord, who is the Spirit" (3 v 18). As we see God's glory, so we reflect God's glory. We are restored as God's image-bearers, reflecting his glory in his world. We give God glory by receiving glory from him and then radiating it back to him.

How do we see the glory of God? The face of Moses, we are told, was radiant not so much because he had seen the LORD but "because he had spoken with the LORD" (Exodus 34 v 29). So it is for us—we see God's glory and receive glory from him through his word.

So Paul goes on in 2 Corinthians 4 to exhort us to press on with the ministry of proclaiming God's word plainly. People don't always respond because, like the Israelites (3 v 14-15), their hearts are veiled (4 v 3). The god of this age has blinded their minds (v 4). But we don't lose heart because the Spirit can remove that blindness. "But," says Paul, "whenever anyone turns to the Lord, the veil is taken away" (3 v 16). The Spirit opens our eyes to see the Lord's glory.

But what is this word that reveals to us the glory of God? What is this word that we are to proclaim so that others might see God's glory? It is "the light of the gospel that displays the glory of Christ, who is the image of God" (4 v 4).

Notice how Paul brings together the ideas of light, glory and image. Christ is the image of God. He is the One who makes the invisible God visible. And Christ is the glory of God. Christ's glory is a perfect reflection of God's glory because Christ is God. And so it is in Christ that we see God, and it is in Christ that we see the glory of God.

And how do we see Christ? In "the light of the gospel". The story of salvation with Christ at its centre—the story of Christ's life, death, resurrection and ascension, and the proclamation of Christ by the early church—is where we see the glory of God.

So we preach Christ rather than ourselves, Paul says, "for God, who said, 'Let light shine out of darkness,' made his light shine in our hearts to give us the light of the knowledge of God's glory displayed in the face of Christ" (4 v 6). Moses went up the mountain, spoke with God, encountered his glory and came down radiating glory. We come to Christ. We hear the gospel of Christ. And in that gospel we see Christ. And in Christ we see the glory of God so that the glory of God shines in our hearts.

Christians radiate God's glory just like Moses did, but there is an important difference. The Israelites saw the glory of God reflecting from the face of Moses. But it was only "the end of what was passing away" (3 v 13). We see the glory of God reflecting from "the face of Christ" (4 v 6)—and it doesn't pass away. Not only does it not fade, but in fact we are transformed by "*ever-increasing* glory" (3 v 18). As we grow as Christians, we increasingly see, and show, the glory of God in the glory of Christ in the story of Christ.

## Meditate

*Grace and truth came through Jesus Christ.*

*Silent night, holy night,*
*Son of God, love's pure light;*
*radiant beams from thy holy face*
*with the dawn of redeeming grace,*
*Jesus, Lord, at thy birth,*
*Jesus, Lord, at thy birth.*
*(Silent Night)*

～

## Prayer

*May the LORD bless us*
*and keep us;*
*may the LORD make his face shine on us*
*and be gracious to us;*
*may the LORD turn his face towards us*
*and give us peace.*
*Amen.*
*(Based on Numbers 6 v 24-26)*

# Loved

> "No one has ever seen God, but the one
> and only Son, who is himself God
> and is in the closest relationship with the Father,
> has made him known."
>
> John 1 v 18

We all want to be loved. We want admiration. We want people to be pleased with us. How many times this week have you hoped someone would notice what you've done and commend you for it?

I do this all the time, but in a very subtle way. I don't hog the limelight. I deftly deflect praise. I have a great line in self-deprecation. But all the time I'm hoping people will admire my humility!

The problem is we're not always loveable or admirable or pleasing. And so people's love for us is patchy. Sometimes they're gushing. But sometimes they're distant, frustrated or bitter.

When Jesus was baptised, the voice of his Father from heaven said, "You are my Son, whom I love; with you I am well pleased" (Luke 3 v 22). Jesus is the Beloved. The Father loves him completely, wholly, with no condition or caveat. Why?

Jesus is loved because he is God's Son. The Father and the Son have always existed in love. In his prayer to the Father in John 17 v 24 Jesus says, "You loved me before the creation of the world" (see also 3 v 35; 5 v 20; 15 v 9; 17 v 23).

∾

This trinitarian love is of profound significance. Let me highlight two ways in which it matters.

First, trinitarian love defines the Persons of the Trinity. The Father is the Father because he has a Son. The Son is the Son because he has a Father. And they are united in love through the Spirit. If the Father were to stop loving his Son, then he would stop being the Father.

The first Christians struggled to define the distinctions between the persons of the Trinity (unsurprisingly!). At first, they tried to do it through causation—who caused whom. The Son and the Spirit were described as deriving their divinity from the Father. But this might imply that the Son and the Spirit were inferior, because while the Father was God in himself, they were only divine through the Father.

In the 5th century, Augustine of Hippo defined the Persons of the Trinity in terms of their relationships. The Father is the Father because he has a Son. The Son is the Son because he has a Father. And the Spirit is the love which unites them. The Spirit is, as it were, the emissary who brings them together. The Persons of the Trinity are defined by their relationships, by their love for one another.

Second, trinitarian love is the fountain of all God's purposes. The Father creates and then recreates the world (through raising his Son, saving his people, and sending his Son to judge and renew) because he wants people to share his delight in his Son. He loves his Son and therefore he wants to bring glory to his Son. The

Son participates in creation and recreation because he wants to bring glory to his Father. Likewise the Spirit animates creation and recreation to bring glory to the Father and the Son. The triune Persons mutually delight in one another and create the world to share that delight. They mutually love one another and create a new family to share that love.

It is this trinitarian love at work in recreation that Paul celebrates in his great hymn of praise in Ephesians 1 v 3-14. In turn, he focuses on the work of the Father (v 3-6), the Son (v 7-12) and the Holy Spirit (v 13-14). Each section ends, "to the praise of his glorious grace" or "for the praise of his glory" (v 6, 12, 14). The goal of all God's purposes is the praise of his glory.

This is not self-centred or egotistical. The Father is pursuing the glory of the Son, the Son is pursuing the glory of the Father, and the Spirit is pursuing the glory of the Father and the Son—all because of their mutual love for one another. It is as though they each point to the others and say to creation, and those who live in it, *Look—aren't they glorious? Won't you join with me in praising them?*

The driving force in the universe is love—the love of the triune Persons for one another. Jesus is the Beloved because he is God's Son. And Jesus is the Beloved in whom we are truly loved, having been called into this relationship by each member of the Trinity.

So what do I do when I want admiration or praise? What do I do when I'm not admirable or praise-worthy? I remember that I'm part of the family—the divine family. I'm loved by the Father in the Son. I'm loved whether people notice me or not. I'm loved whether I'm loveable or not. That enables me to cope with criticism. It enables me to cope with failure. After all, I'm loved in the Beloved. I'm in the closest relationship with the Father for I share the closeness of the Son.

*Tim Chester*

## Meditate

*The one and only Son, who is himself God
and is in the closest relationship with the Father...*

*All creation, join in praising God the Father, Spirit, Son,
Evermore your voices raising, To th'eternal Three in One:*
*(Angels from the Realms of Glory)*

∾

## Prayer

*Father God, we praise you for your glorious grace.
For you have blessed us in the heavenly realms
with every spiritual blessing in Christ.
For you chose us in him before the creation of the world
to be holy and blameless in your sight.
In love you predestined us for adoption to sonship through Jesus Christ.*

*Jesus Christ, we praise you for your glorious grace.
For in you we have redemption through your blood,
the forgiveness of sins,
in accordance with the riches of God's grace that he lavished on us.
And God has made known to us the mystery of his will:
to bring unity to all things in heaven and on earth under you.*

*Holy Spirit, we praise you for your glorious grace.
For we were included in Christ
when we heard the message of truth, the gospel of salvation.
You are a seal, the mark that we belong to Christ.
You are a deposit, the guarantee of our inheritance,
until the redemption of those who are God's possession. Amen.*
*(Based on Ephesians 1 v 3-14)*

# The altogether lovely

*"The one and only Son,
who is himself God and is in the closest relationship
with the Father,
has made him known."*
John 1 v 18

A *ltogether lovely.* Jesus is the "altogether lovely" One. That's a quote from Song of Songs 5 v 16. There, it describes the beloved Lover. But throughout the Bible, the relationship between a husband and wife is a pointer to Christ's relationship to his bride, the church. Jesus is the husband who is altogether lovely.

As we have seen, Jesus is the Beloved because he is God's Son. But he is also loved by God the Father because he's lovely. Think about how we see this in the life of Jesus.

Jesus is lovely in his compassion. "When Jesus landed and saw a large crowd, he had compassion on them, because they were like sheep without a shepherd" (Mark 6 v 34). We are, as it were, part of that crowd. When Jesus looks on you, he looks on you with compassion.

Jesus is lovely in his patience. Think of how slow the disciples are to grasp who he is. When they recognise him as the Messiah, they're then slow to realise this means he must suffer and die. Three times in Mark's Gospel, Jesus predicts his sufferings and death. After the first time, Peter rebukes him. After the other two occasions, the disciples immediately get into an argument about which of them is the greatest. In the end, they all betray him. Yet in John 20, Jesus greets these flawed, failing friends of his with a simple word: "Peace" (v 9). In John 21, Jesus gently restores Peter. What patience! We experience the patience of Jesus ourselves. We're often like sheep wandering from the path. But Jesus patiently restores us.

Jesus is lovely in his gentleness. We see this in his attitude to those battered by society. He has time for children. He touches lepers. He cares for the poor. He welcomes the outcast. He treats women with dignity. Quoting from Isaiah 42 v 1-4, Matthew's summary of the ministry of Jesus includes these words: "He will not quarrel or cry out; no one will hear his voice in the streets. A bruised reed he will not break, and a smouldering wick he will not snuff out" (Matthew 12 v 19-20).

Jesus is lovely in his anger. He is always angry for the right reasons in the right way. His anger is never petulant, selfish or uncontrolled. In Mark 3 v 1-6 the religious leaders bring a man with a shrivelled hand to Jesus. They care nothing for the man. They simply want to trap Jesus. Jesus is angry at their indifference. His anger is lovely because it's the response of his love to evil.

Jesus is lovely in his justice. He always does what is right. He can't be manipulated. He's not susceptible to pressure or privilege. As he stands trial before the Sanhedrin and then before Pilate, it becomes clear that in fact they are the ones being judged.

Above all, Jesus is lovely in his love. We see his love throughout his life, but the great demonstration of his love is the cross. And the

Father loves him because of this love: "The reason my Father loves me is that I lay down my life—only to take it up again" (John 10 v 17).

∾

The Father loves the Son because eternally the Son has submitted to the Father's will in love. Jesus didn't earn the Father's love at the cross. The Father and Son have always lived in love, with the Son living with the obedience of a child towards his Father. The cross is the supreme expression of that obedience.

The reason the Father loves Jesus is that Jesus is the kind of Son who so loves his Father and so loves his people that he is prepared to lay down his life. Jesus is the Beloved because he is God's Son and because he is lovely.

And remember—you and I are children of God through Christ. The Father loves us with the same love that he has for his Son. Jesus is the Beloved in whom we are truly loved.

## Meditate

*Jesus is ... in the closest relationship with the Father...*

*Why lies he in such mean estate,*
*Where ox and donkeys are feeding?*
*Good Christians, fear, for sinners here*
*The silent Word is pleading.*

*Nails, spears shall pierce him through,*
*the cross he bore for me, for you.*
*Hail, hail the Word made flesh,*
*the Babe, the Son of Mary.*
*(What Child is This?)*

## Prayer

*O Lover to the uttermost,*
*may I read the meltings of thy heart to me,*
*in the manger of thy birth,*
*in the garden of thy agony,*
*in the cross of thy suffering,*
*in the tomb of thy resurrection,*
*in the heaven of thy intercession …*
*Thou hast loved me everlastingly, unchangeably,*
*may I love thee as I am loved;*
*thou hast given thyself for me,*
*may I give myself to thee;*
*thou hast died for me,*
*may I live to thee,*
*in every moment of my time,*
*in every movement of my mind,*
*in every pulse of my heart.*
*Amen.*

*(From "Christ is All" in The Valley of Vision )*

# Where I am

*"In closest relationship with the Father..."*
John 1 v 18

As a parent, having a small child of yours crawl into your bed and snuggle into you is a wonderful feeling. My daughters used to do it every morning. It's probably a good thing they grew out of it—they're not as small as they used to be, nor as cute. But I do miss it.

I remember that experience as a father—sadly, I can't remember what it was like to be a child snuggling into the arms of my own father. But the daily burrowing of my daughters under the duvet provided plenty of evidence that children enjoy the closeness it brings.

How similar is your view of your relationship with the Creator of every atom to this picture of the delighted, tender father and the contented, secure child? In Christ, we are loved by a heavenly Father. So the answer can be, and should be: *Very* similar.

God loves us in Christ. And Christ is always and altogether

lovely. And so God's love for us in his Beloved is guaranteed. Jesus is the Beloved in whom we are truly loved. God can no more stop loving us than he can stop loving his Son.

∽

The word "advent" means "coming". During the season of Advent we remember the coming of Jesus—and that, of course, means we need to remember two comings—his first coming and his second coming. For in John 14 v 3, Jesus promises, "I will come back and take you to be with me that you also may be where I am".

At his first advent, Jesus came to be where we are. At his second advent, he will come so that we can be where he is. This was his prayer on the night before he died: "Father, I want those you have given me to be with me where I am, and to see my glory, the glory you have given me because you loved me before the creation of the world" (17 v 24).

Jesus wants his people to be where he is. So where is that? God "the one and only Son, who is himself God and is in the closest relationship with the Father, has made him known" (1 v 18). The Son is in the "closest relationship" with the Father—literally, "on his chest" or "in his bosom". Jesus wants his people to lie on God's chest. It's the image of a child snuggled up on her father's lap. Jesus has come so that we can be children of God; so that we can feel the arms of God wrap around us; so that we can share that closest of relationships with God.

∽

As he prayed the night before he died, Jesus continued, "Righteous Father, though the world does not know you, I know you, and they know that you have sent me. I have made you known to them, and will continue to make you known in order that the love you have for me may be in them and that I myself may be in them" (17 v 25).

Jesus knows the Father; and now Jesus has made the Father known to his disciples. Jesus is loved by the Father; and now Jesus has made the Father known to us as our Father, so that the Father's love may be in us.

When Jesus promises to come back so we can be where he is, he adds, "You know the way to the place where I am going" (14 v 4). Thomas replies, "Lord, we don't know where you are going, so how can we know the way?" (v 5). Famously, Jesus replied, "I am the way and the truth and the life. No one comes to the Father except through me" (v 6). Jesus is the way and his place with the Father—his relationship with his Father in the home of his Father—is the destination.

Look to Jesus the Beloved—that is the love the Father has for you. Look at his relationship with the Father—that is the relationship the Father has with you. Look to where Jesus is—that is where you are heading.

That's a recipe for a truly happy Christmas.

## Meditate
*I will come back and take you to be with me*
*that you also may be where I am.*

*Now redemption, long expected,*
*See in solemn pomp appear:*
*All his saints, by men rejected,*
*Now shall meet him in the air:*
*Alleluia! Alleluia!*
*See the day of God appear.*
*(Lo! He Comes with Clouds Descending)*

∽

## Prayer
*Come, my Way, my Truth, my Life:*
*such a Way, as gives us breath:*
*such a Truth, as ends all strife:*
*such a Life, as killeth death.*

*Come, my Light, my Feast, my Strength:*
*such a Light, as shows a feast:*
*such a Feast, as mends in length:*
*such a Strength, as makes his guest.*

*Come, my Joy, my Love, my Heart:*
*such a Joy, as none can move:*
*such a Love, as none can part:*
*such a Heart, as joys in love.*
*("The Call" by George Herbert, 1593-1633)*

# The one and only Son

*"The one and only Son ...
has made him known."*
John 1 v 18

Have you ever wished you could see God? That's what Philip wanted. In John 14 v 8 this disciple of Jesus says, "Lord, show us the Father and that will be enough for us". Perhaps you share Philip's feelings. Seeing God would make all the difference. You would have so much more confidence in the truth, so much more commitment to obedience. Or perhaps you've met people like Philip, who say to you, "Show us God. Give us some evidence. You talk about God. Well, show me your God."

This is how Jesus replies: "Don't you know me, Philip, even after I have been among you such a long time? Anyone who has seen me has seen the Father. How can you say, 'Show us the Father'?" (v 9).

To see Jesus is to see God the Father. When we introduce people to Jesus, we are introducing them to God. "The one and only Son ... has made him known."

In Colossians 1 v 15, Paul says, "The Son is the image of the invisible God". Jesus is the image of God. Jesus makes visible the God who is invisible. Jesus images God. He is a living photograph of God.

The writer of Hebrews says he is "the exact representation of his being" (1 v 3). Jesus exactly represents God. Think of Jesus as God's self-portrait. If a great artist paints a self-portrait, then you might say, "It reflects his likeness and captures his personality". God is the greatest artist. His self-portrait in Jesus perfectly reflects his likeness and exactly captures his personality. Indeed so exactly does Jesus image God that Jesus is God. There is no difference between them except that Jesus is the image and the Father is the imaged.

What have we seen of Jesus in these opening verses of John's Gospel? We have seen, as it were, various pieces of the portrait. Now, as we finish, we need to pause, step back, and appreciate what the whole picture looks like.

- **Jesus is the true Adam**, who has come to recreate our humanity.

- **Jesus is the true God**, the uncreated Creator God.

- **Jesus is the Word**, through whom we hear the voice of God.

- **Jesus is the Word,** through whom God created the world and through whom God is recreating the world.

- **Jesus is the One who has been given life** in himself so he can give life to his people.

- **Jesus is the true light**, who enlightens our minds and lights up our lives.

- **Jesus is the point at which heaven and earth intersect.**

- **Jesus is God-in-the-flesh**: deity squeezed into human form.

- **Jesus is divine wisdom**, love, holiness, justice, truth in human form.

- **Jesus is God among us**, God's address on earth.

- **Jesus is the glory of God**, the embodiment of all his perfections.

- **Jesus is God's native language,** the Word we encounter in the Bible.

- **Jesus is the way home to God.**

- **Jesus is the King** who cares for us, the Bread who satisfies us and the Light who guides us.

- **Jesus is the radiance of God**, whose glory transforms us as we gaze upon him.

- **Jesus is the Son of God**, in whom we experience the love of the Father.

- **Jesus is the altogether lovely One** who brings us into the loving arms of his Father.

What is the picture of God that emerges from the image or "photograph" we see of him in Jesus? What have we discovered about God in "the one and only Son", who "has made him known"?

We have seen that Jesus is the eternal Son of God—he was with God and was God. And, because Jesus is God, he perfectly reveals God the Father. And at the instigation of the Father, Jesus has come as the world's Creator to be the beginning of the recreation of the world. Just as God gave life to the physical creation, so God now through Jesus brings life to those who are spiritually dead. God is rewriting the story of this world through Jesus. And he can rewrite our life stories, too.

We have seen, too, that Jesus connects earth and heaven. He is the bridge between God and humanity. Through Jesus we are introduced to the Father. We look at God and see not simply a terrifying Judge, but a loving Father. Indeed, we are loved with the same love that the Father has for his Son. We are born anew as God's children.

We have seen that in Jesus God has come to live among us. And God's presence among us in Jesus means we experience glory—radiant, transforming glory. We see divine perfections. We receive divine love.

For a few moments, slowly read through the last two pages, from the first "Jesus is..." As you're led to, pause and praise the God who has made himself known in his Son. Write down which of these truths has captured your heart as we have looked at John 1. Reflect on which of these truths is changing your life. Enjoy identifying how this Christmas will be more meaningful and more joyful for you because, in the middle of everything else that is going on, you have gazed at the One in the manger—the one and only Son.

## Meditate

*The one and only Son ... has made him known.*

*Good Christian men, rejoice*
*With heart and soul and voice!*
*Now ye need not fear the grave:*
*Peace! Peace!*
*Jesus Christ was born to save.*
*Calls you one and calls you all,*
*To gain his everlasting hall;*
*Christ was born to save!*
*Christ was born to save!*
*(Good Christian Men, Rejoice)*

ᕲ

## Prayer

*Immortal, invisible, God only wise,*
*In light inaccessible hid from our eyes,*
*Most blessèd, most glorious, the Ancient of Days,*
*Almighty, victorious, thy great Name we praise ...*
*All laud we would render; O help us to see*
*Tis only the splendour of light hideth thee,*
*And so let thy glory, Almighty, impart,*
*Through Christ in his story, thy Christ to the heart.*
*(Walter Chalmers Smith, 1824-1908)*

# More from thegoodbook
COMPANY

## A Very Different Christmas
**Rico Tice and Nate Morgan Locke**

An intriguingly different introduction to Christianity which invites readers to open Christmas gifts from the Father, Son and Holy Spirit. Ideal for giving away in the holiday season. Buy it, read it, give it away!

ISBN: 9781784980146

### 5 Things To Pray For The People You Love
**Rachel Jones**
ISBN: 9781910307397

### 5 Things To Pray For Your Church
**Rachel Jones**
ISBN: 9781784980306

Two books of practical help and encouragement that are crammed with ideas and fresh Bible perspectives to breathe new life into your prayers.

**thegoodbook.co.uk  thegoodbook.com**